WORDS

of Inspiration

A QUIET MESSAGE FOR THE SOUL

RHONDA BERRY

AuthorHouse™
1663 Liberty Drive
Bloomington, IN 47403
www.authorhouse.com
Phone: 833-262-8899

Because of the dynamic nature of the Internet, any web addresses or links contained in this book may have changed since publication and may no longer be valid. The views expressed in this work are solely those of the author and do not necessarily reflect the views of the publisher, and the publisher hereby disclaims any responsibility for them.

Any people depicted in stock imagery provided by Getty Images are models, and such images are being used for illustrative purposes only. Certain stock imagery © Getty Images.

This book is printed on acid-free paper.

ISBN: 978-1-6655-7894-3 (sc)
ISBN: 978-1-6655-7893-6 (e)

Library of Congress Control Number: 2022923791

Print information available on the last page.

Published by AuthorHouse 03/17/2023

authorHOUSE

Contents

Dedication...5

Acknowledgements..6

Child of the Almighty King..7

Encouragement..9

You Will See Me Again...10

Exercise Faith..12

When God Speaks...13

People May Say...15

Today I Will Smile..17

Keep Moving On..19

Just Try..20

You Can Make It Through..22

Affirmation..23

You Are A Vision..24

See Yourself as God Sees You..25

Mother of Zion..26

The Amazing Wonderful Woman.......................................28

Made to Be You...30

I Always Win...31

Inspiration...33

Glad To See One More Day...34

Morning Praise..35

In His Presence...36

God's Grace...37

Use Your Talent...38

Shine Your Light..39

Negative Thoughts...40

I'm Better..41

Salvation...42

Preachers, Preach!...44

Reflection..46

You Will See Me Again 47
Exercise Faith 48
When God Speaks 49
People May Say 50
Today I Will Smile 51
Keep Moving On 52
Just Try 53
You Can Make It Through 54
You Are A Vision 55
See Yourself As God Sees You 56
Mother of Zion 57
The Amazing Wonderful Woman 58
Made To Be You 59
I Always Win 60
Glad To See One More Day 61
Morning Praise 62
In His Presence 63
God's Grace 65
Use Your Talents 67
Shine Your Light 69
Negative Thoughts 70
I'm Better 72
Salvation 73

Words from the Heart
A Message from the Author 74
About the Author 75

Dedication

In honor of my late Grandfather, Reverend Russell Roosevelt Jones Sr. Granddad, as a little girl I often heard the stories of your character - how quiet, nice and kind you were. But most intriguing to me was hearing the story of your faith. Especially the story of when your son, was stillborn how you told the doctor to bring him to you, and you prayed until life came back into him.

Because of your faith and acceptance to the call of God and relentless prayers for your children, generations of ministry gifts were birthed within our family line. I am a product of your prayers.

Thank you, Granddad, for accepting God's call and praying for me.

I also dedicate this book to my lovely mother, Faye Berry, who has been my inspiration and a model example of God's love, and an excellent parent all of my life.

Love you, Mom!

Acknowledgements

First and foremost, to my Lord and Savior Jesus Christ, to whom I give all the honor and glory. I love you Lord!

Thank you, Bishop Marvin Winans, for all that you have imparted into me and the many prayers that you've prayed over me throughout the years. I'm so blessed to have you as my spiritual father and the caretaker of my soul.

Special thanks to Elder Roy Haynes, Elder Willie Ginyard, Marilyn Byrd, Roberta McCoy, and Brenda Johnson for all of your guidance, support, and words of encouragement. It meant a lot to me.

To my family, Faye Berry, Taunji Moore, Lorissa Berry, Jacqueline Hill, and

Gary Hearn. You are the Best! Thanks for everything. I love you guys.

Thank You, to all of my Special Prayer Warriors who encouraged, supported and most of all prayed for me throughout this process – Sharon Barkley, Abena Cabbil, Sheila Ellis, and Laurene Sanders.

Child of the Almighty King

You are a child of the Most High God
Redeemed by the blood of his dear Son
He took on the battle of sin and He won
His work on the cross can never be undone

Because of his great love for you,
Your sins have been forgiven this much is true
You are now free,
To live the new life he created for you

His love is free
Nothing needs to be done
As a Child of the King
Your new life has begun

You are renewed in the spirit
chosen and accepted in the beloved
as a new creation
You will begin to speak the truth directly from the King above

Seated with Christ Jesus in Heavenly places
A Child of the King, royal diadem and an heir to the throne
A citizen of heaven will now be your eternal home

You'll be in the presence of Jesus and the angels too
And an unworthy look may come over you
But Jesus will say "no such thing is true"
Enter into the Gate...
I've Been waiting for you

And before Him they will bring you just as you are
And He will show you your worth in His every scar
And angels will rejoice and sing
Because YOU are a Child of the Almighty King!

Galatians 4:7

Encouragement

You Will See Me Again
(A Message for Grieving Hearts)

I'm sorry my loves
I had to go this way
When I heard the Master's call
I could no longer stay

It was a hard decision for me to make
Because your hearts I never wanted to break
I knew that God would not put more on you than you could bear
So I lovingly left you in his care

The many prayers I stored up for you day and night
Gave me confidence to know that God is holding you now
with all His might
I know happiness will return to you one day
But for now just remember me in your special way
Don't cry for me because I'm gone
I've entered into my eternal home

I'm happy now
I don't have a burden or a care
Up here we praise and magnify God
His praise is everywhere
I can hardly wait for you to enter in too
Here eternal life will began for you
You will take your place where the angels sing
And we will be together forever as we magnify our King
So smile my Loves,
Don't worry about a thing
I'm in heaven where the Angels sing

Be strong and committed until the end
That day our hearts will finally mend
For on that Great and Glorious Day
You will see me again and I will be with you to stay
The trumpet will sound
And I will rise
You will look up and see me with Jesus coming through the skies

Tears of joy will fill your eyes
And we will have a great reunion in the sky

You will See Me Again!

1 Thessalonians 4:16-17

Exercise Faith

I'm reaching for those things
I once thought I couldn't achieve
Because my faith has taught me
I can have anything
If I only believe

Faith is opposite of doubt
It's a sure thing
When coupled with prayer and God's Word
Powerful results it will bring

God is the essence of the faith that I receive
So I stand on His Word and believe what I read
As I plant in my heart every seed
Doubt tries to come in and change what I believe
But I look at doubt and tell it:
Me... you will not deceive

I hold on to my faith by doing things
I thought I couldn't achieve
Yet, knowing by Faith I will receive
I'm believing in the evidence of things unseen
No matter how impossible or how long it may seem

Hebrews 11: 1

When God Speaks

When God speaks...
Miraculous things happen
Day separates from night
Seas split,
Stars began to shine
Life is given to all mankind

At the behest of his Word
All creation must stop and listen
There's power in God's Word
And it happens as He mentions
And He does all things with good intentions

By the authority of his Word
The world came into existence
And everything was created just as he envisioned and just as He said
Mountains moved, Birds flew
Seas roared, Winds blew
Then God created me and you

When God speaks...
His Word does as He commands
All creation is subservient to Him in every nation and land
Every tongue will confess his Lordship as the Word demands
He's GOD and when He speaks, He will fulfill His every plan

When God speaks...
All creation will bow to the one True God
Angels sing Hallelujah adorning him with praise
Men kneel in reverence with their hands raised

When God speaks...

Satan and demons run and tremble
And their works are defeated and totally disassembled
His Word is final and it is true
He is not a human like me and you

He cannot lie or have to repent
He's God of all creation
And His Word responds as it is sent

Isaiah 55:11

People May Say

People may say that you're NOT...

Good
Pretty
Smart
Talented
Courageous
or
Confident enough

They may even say that they don't like you very much
Or that they don't want to be around you or such
Don't let the negative things that people say cloud your view
Discourage, hinder or make you feel blue
God knows everything that he placed inside of you
And you can do anything that you set your mind to do
Their words are not only not true,
But they are jealous because God made you, YOU!

You are so much more than what they have to say
Believe instead that you are the beautiful portrait that he portrays
God said No weapon formed against you shall prosper
God made you real and not an imposter
Stop worrying about what other people say
Let them say what they say!
And let God have His Way!

Because guess what! They didn't create you anyway
So they can't add or take anything away
So, when people have negative things to say
Erase what they say without delay
As you smile and continue on your merry way

It's the Word that God pronounced over you
that you must listen to and obey
God made you special inside and out like a beautiful bouquet

For it is His Word that is emphatically true
It's His Words that will carry you through
And it's His Word that lives inside of You!

Romans 3:4

Today I Will Smile

Today I will smile
Come what may
My smile is lovely and here to stay
When I smile
Cares and worries...they fade away
Sadness and gloom, not today!

A smile on me
brightens up my day
and causes others to smile
who are passing my way

A smile is contagious!
Try it! You'll see!
My smile will make you smile
It's a guarantee!
The more you smile
The more smiles you'll see

I won't let the cares of life
take away my beautiful smile
It's not worth it
Not even for a little while

My smile shows I don't let people and things weigh me down
My smile brings joy and cheerfulness around
A smile can lift you when you're feeling sad or blue
No one wants a frown around...
Do you?

I'm glad that I chose to smile today
It chased my cares and worries away
So if you're feeling down
Smile on purpose and you'll see
How much brighter your day will be!

Today I Will Smile!

Proverbs 15:13

Keep Moving On

We all have aspirations and dreams that we are trying to attain
Sometimes they look like a mountain or a road too far to obtain
When we look far ahead
That's when we face our goals that seem so lifeless and dead
But with persistence and determination, we will achieve
We become victors if we keep moving on and believe

Your mountain may look enormous
The road may seem long
At times you may get weary
But keep moving on
The steps you take may seem really small now
You really are moving, as fast as God will allow
Small steps or giant steps you're advancing as you go
Just keep moving on because you're more resilient than you know

With each step a new victory is gained
Toward your goal you are moving and it's being attained
As you move towards your goal, the size of your mountain
does become smaller
It does not remain the same and it does not get taller
So, be steadfast and unmovable
Always looking and moving ahead
Until you're standing on top of your mountain
looking down at the road you no longer dread

Look back at what you've accomplished, you've conquered
the mountain top
Don't let anything discourage you from now on or cause you to stop
Be confident that there's nothing you can't achieve
Stay determined, keep moving, and most importantly – believe!

1 Corinthians 15:58

Just Try

If you have a gift that you've been told
Step out and use it and be very bold
Be courageous in the midst of your fears
Although at times you may shed secret tears

Your gift will not completely develop overnight
So, roll up your sleeves, go to work, and burn the midnight light
Perfecting your gift may seem really challenging to do
Take the challenge, and let your gift come through

Persevere when your gift is not accepted
Learn from the constructive criticism
It doesn't mean that your gift is rejected
It will only help you perfect it

It may hurt for now, and you may feel the strain
But the pain of your labor won't remain
Things come to life when we push through
And your gift will be birthed right out of you

The pain you feel is to make you stronger
So don't quit
Hold on to your gift a little while longer
If you don't try
You'll never know what you can do
Or see the manifestation of God's gifts inside of you

If you don't try
You'll never develop your gift
Or see how many people it can uplift
Don't give up because you feel you've failed
If you keep working at it you will prevail

When you finish trying "get up and do"
Because with Christ all things are possible for you
Have confidence in the gift that you have been given
Don't let the challenges cause your gift to be hidden

Philippians 4:13

You Can Make It Through

When times seem hard and you feel like you're in a storm
Lean on Him and watch Him perform
There's nothing too difficult for him to do
There's never a problem He won't see you through
God's strength can transform anything that seems like a thorn
God has been watching over you since you were born

He will lighten your burdens and lift up your heart
With the extraordinary love that only he can impart
God is working out his best in you
Doing what only He can do
So, let your praises be many and never few
If you wait on him, you can make it through

Don't become fretful or weary and believe it's untrue
Keep looking forward and walk on to pursue
His promises, purposes and plans all anew
For in your storm a blessing is being prepared exclusively for you
Hold your head up high and march on through!

Psalms 107:29

Affirmation

You Are A Vision

You are a vision of the Master's plan
A blueprint of your life he carefully designed with his hand
He is the potter and you are the clay
He shaped and designed you according to his wonderful way

It may be hard for some to comprehend
But everything about you is as he intends
You were predestined before your life and your journey began
Because he chose to love you your entire life span

He knows the thoughts that he has towards you
And the path he laid out, he already knew
Therefore, walk in your calling, fulfill the Master's Plan
For you are a masterpiece created by God's hand

Jeremiah 29:11

See Yourself as God Sees You

When you see yourself as God sees you
You're far more valuable, precious and worthy than you ever knew
The most expensive price was paid when God's Son gave His life for you
He freed you from all sin, guilt and shame
And your life He forever changed

Nothing about you remains the same
You can now live a new life and not be ashamed
There is nothing for the devil to give God as your blame
You have been transformed and given a brand-new name

There's a beauty inside of you that now exists
And a light that shines so bright that it cannot be missed,
Your eternal light is hard to resist
See yourself as God's precious gift

You are a perfect reflection of God's love and affection
Created in His image to give Him Glory
When the world looks at you, they see His perfect love story
You are part of God's selected inventory

So See Yourself As God Sees You
You're more special and royal than what you knew
God made you in His image when he made you anew
So See yourself today as God sees you

1 Peter 2:9

Mother of Zion
In honor of Mother Ruth (Melissa Davis) 100th birthday celebration

She has power in the words that she speaks
Yet in her spirit she is humble, gentle and meek
You will hear years of wisdom and experience talk
About Mother's Faith and Godly walk

Holiness is the life that she lives
And love is the fruit that she freely gives
She strengthens her faith with prayer when times get rough
And her steadfastness and determination never allows her to give up

She's certain that God called her and summoned her to preach
He has anointed her to lay hands, to bless, prophesy, and to teach
Her assignment from God, she is determined to reach
Nothing will stand in her way
Not today or any other day
Because she's strong like a lion
This Mother of Zion
Yet, meek as a dove
From heaven above

Through tribulations, struggles, tests, and trials
She prays and with faith, she continues to smile
She touches, reaches and saves many souls
With the Holy boldness and the Word of God that she upholds

She is full of godly character, integrity and strength
And she never wavered to give God her tenth
As he rewarded her with a life full of blessings and with long length

She leads by the example that she lives and she gives
She teaches women how to stand firm in the Lord
And how to live righteous, for there is a reward

She teaches how to combat all of the enemy's plans
And how to live safely in the Master's hands
Oh yes, through the years she has shed many tears
And fought with faith, many anxieties and fears
But her impeccable faith has sustained her through it all
And when faced with trouble, to her knees she did fall

This Mother of Zion was polished with grace
And equipped by God to run this Christian race
And it carried her through into her heavenly place
And now Mother is resting peacefully in God's loving embrace

Oh Mother of Zion!
Psalms 92:13-14, Titus 2:3-4

The Amazing Wonderful Woman
(A Poem for Self-Esteem)

When God created woman he put his best ingredients into her
He took his time and pondered on how he wanted her to be
He decided to make her beautiful inside and out
For the whole world to see

God saw that man was lonely
So he made someone for him and him only
From the rib of Adam the first woman came
And after Eve God made no two exactly the same
God created the woman uniquely beautiful inside and out
He made her perfect for man without a doubt

There was none like her throughout the land
And she was quite opposite of Adam, the man
God had made Adam tough, rough and strong inside
In her is where helpfulness, sweetness and gentleness reside
She is also smart, warm, sensitive, loving and kind
She even has the ability to change the world, you will find

God also thought intensively about how he wanted her to look
He gave woman her feminine fullness
along with beautiful skin, hair and eyes
Long legs, hips and beautiful thighs
Out of his own vision, he grafted and formed her shape
God made her wonderful and amazing and without any mistake
When God created woman, he created her out of the love of his heart
He filled her with emotions and gave her a special way that sets her apart

When God created the woman, she was the gentler part of man
Created to help him fulfill the Master's plan
So God gave Eve as Adam's wife
To create and multiply and to add more life

The first time man laid eyes on her,
He found no dissatisfaction
He had a wonderful reaction and an instant attraction
Adam saw the beauty she had inside
Natural beauty, you just can't hide

Woman! Like Eve, you were created "Wonderful" right from the start
You are God's masterpiece and work of art
You are fearfully and wonderfully made
Special to God, and a unique gift to man
More valuable than the world could ever comprehend
Wonderful Woman you are so amazing!
You were created just as God planned

Psalms 139: 14

Made to Be You

You were made to be exactly who you are
There's no one else in the world who can ever be like you
Nor, do the exceptional things that you are called to do
God created and made you extraordinary
You're far better than just ordinary

You are one of a kind
A person like you is "so" hard to find
You're in a class all by yourself
Filled with elegance, flair and so much style
Wow! Look at you!
You have so many reasons to smile

Hold on to your uniqueness, you are a Star
Enjoy being different, you're better off by far
Trying to be like someone else, "well that's just bizarre"
Because you're magnificent just as you are

The world needs you and the gifts and talents you possess
Stop trying to be like all of the rest
When God made you, he made you the best
God didn't create you like anyone else
He made you to be you, one of a kind
Another you, the world will not find

So, don't hide what you have inside
You're made to be you to grow and to thrive
You're made to be you, let your gifts come alive
Be the best that you can be for the whole world to see
And know that you're special and exceptional to me

"Made to be you"

Jeremiah 1:5; 29:11

I Always Win

Get off my back Satan
You are always bothering me
But I have been set free, way back on Calvary
You ought to know, you don't run this show
You have no power, you evil devour

All strongholds were broken
When the Word was spoken
Jesus canceled my debt of sin
He said "I Always Win"

I've been purchased by God
Bought with the blood of the lamb
So, all your sneaky, cunning tactics
Have already been condemned

With the Word of God and my shield in my hand
I tear down, cancel and destroy all of your wicked plans
I rebuke you Satan, in Jesus' name
You have come to an open shame
Because when I call on His name,
Nothing remains the same

Now flee! Let me be!
You have no power or control over me
By the blood of Jesus, I have been set free
He fought the battle
He won it for me
Jesus gave me the victory

Throw your best shot
Give it all you got

Your weapons can't hurt me, They can't even form
He paid for my sin, Before I was born
God prepared me to win
He gave me the power over sin

I'm no longer a sinner
I am now a winner
Because of Him I always win

Colossians 2:15

Inspiration

Glad To See One More Day

Every morning when I arise
I'll stretch forth my hands and lift them toward the skies
Thankful to God for the new mercies that I see
And the Blessing of a new day of life He has bestowed upon me

His Word says to rejoice and be glad in this day
For me I wouldn't start it out any other way
The spirit of happiness and peace is all around
Because the joy that Jesus put into my life is so profound

Praises and songs are flowing through my heart today
Because God has allowed me to live to see one more day
Death could have come and took my life from me
But God blocked it, and He told death "you have to flee"
Happy am I to be in the land of the living
To have one more day, to give God thanksgiving

I am so grateful for each day that I arise
I get so excited, you can see it in my eyes
When I view the new horizons in God's blue skies
And view the endless possibilities and opportunities for me to take
Blessed that death is not my ultimate fate
These new opportunities, I will not forsake
Each and Every day that I awake

I am so delighted that God had His way
Very excited and very blessed to say
"I'm Glad To Be Here One More Day!"

Psalms 118:24

Morning Praise

Early in the morning, I wake up and see
The brand new day that the Lord has given to me
I rise each new day to bow and to praise him too
For new mercy, new grace and new blessings anew
I magnify his Holy name before the sun rises high
My praise song shall rise above to thee in the sky

I'll pour out my heart in worship to Jesus Christ my King
To him I will lift up my voice as I joyfully sing
I'll praise him for his goodness
His mercy, his love, and his grace
And thank him for another day of life that I gratefully embrace
My heart shall sing praises adoring him with love
As I give worship to the one and true Savior seated in heaven above

Psalms 5:1-3

In His Presence

In the presence of God is the Holy place
Where my soul seeks to see His glorious face
In His Presence is where I will live
My heart to him, I freely give
In his presence I go daily without delay
Quickly I fall to my knees and pray
To give honor and thanks to the Lord today
For blessing and allowing me in His presence another day

In His presence I hear his gentle voice speak to my heart
From his presence I have no desire to ever depart
In His Presence I often feel his hand on mine
Guiding and protecting me on the path he defines
Every day that I wake, he gives me a fresh new start
And he showers me with blessings that only he can impart

Oh, what joy he brings to my soul
For by his love
I have been made whole
In the presence of God is where I desire to be
Because I'm confident that's where he hears and answers me

1 Chronicles 16:27-29

God's Grace

If you fall into sin or you missed the mark
Repent of your wrong doing and ask God to cleanse your heart
Don't let sin stop you or make you feel disgraced
You can come boldly to the Father at His throne of grace
There you will obtain God's mercy, find his favor and a repenting space
He will welcome you with arms wide open and your sins He will replace
With his safe, loving and forgiving embrace

Forgiveness is yours if your heart is sincere
When you cry out to the Lord, he will certainly hear
God will not turn away from you if you have a broken and a contrite heart
But from your wrong doing you must definitely depart

If you don't stop, the repercussions of your sin will cost you a lot
That's the devil's plan and his plot
To keep you believing you are bound but you're not
The blood of Jesus cleansed you from every blemish and every spot
So hold on to the victory over sin that you got

Don't let the enemy trick you and cause you to sin
By doing the same thing over and over again
You are a new creature, leave the past behind
You now have a new life that has been specifically designed
The guilt and shame you feel at times can make you feel confined
But you are justified by Faith in Jesus as your Savior
And not by your labor or behavior
God's Grace has covered you completely with His love and His favor

Hebrews 4:16

Use Your Talent

If you have a talent
Use what you got
Don't hide it under a bushel
Thinking it's too small and not worth a lot

Your talent is a gift from God created for you to use
To give to others and not remain recluse
When you place your talent in the Master's hands
It begins to expand larger than your intended plans

Use your talent and watch your fruit increase
As long as you use your talent for God, your fruit will never cease
So, don't let discouragement and disappointment set in
Use your God given talent and watch your blessings begin
Remember, you will be judged on what you do with your talent, my friend
Use Your Talent and let your creativity begin
We are held accountable for our gifts and talents in the end
And we must use them as God intends

Matthew 25:14-30

Shine Your Light

It's a perplexing world that we're living in
How did it start?
Where did it begin?
This world is full of every sin

People today are looking for hope each and every day
Because so much is going on in the world today
People are lost and simply trying to find their way
You hold the key that the world needs
So open up your heart as the Lord leads

How you may ask
So, let's consider the task
People seem to have lost their way
You need to tell them that Jesus holds the answer
That the world needs today
But they must trust him, listen and obey

You are the light that they seek in the dark
Open up your heart and help show them your spark
Let your light shine brightly each day
Until they find Jesus on their own pathway

You are the salt of the earth, full of flavor, never bland
You're a bright light shining in a very dark land
Share your testimony of Jesus in a way that people will understand
Be the example that the world will know and to see
Let your light shine as an example of what it's like to be free
Let your light tell them that God loved them before the world began
And in their future he has prepared for them a perfect plan

Matthew 5:14-16

Negative Thoughts

I got up early one morning
So many thoughts were going through my head
I couldn't remember anything that anyone had said
Then I shook myself and I asked
"What's the matter with me?"
I'm not going to be bound by these negative thoughts
No, I'm going to be free
I said "Negative thoughts you have to flee
I don't want you living inside of me"

I got down on my knees and I began to pray
Father, take all of these thoughts and cares away
I began to thank God as He changed the course of my day
As I began to think on things according to His way

God said "Think on things that are lovely, admirable, honest, just and pure
I filled my mind with these and the other thoughts had became obscure

Yes, I was free!
Negative thoughts could no longer control me
With prayers they were driven away
They weren't able to take over my day
Not even in the smallest way
Victory happens when we meditate on good things like love
And we pray and wholeheartedly trust in God above

Philippians 4:8, Proverbs 23:7

I'm Better

Things just keep getting better for me
Since I met the man named Jesus who set me free
My outlook on life has been clearer, you see
From the day that Jesus took hold of me

The world inside me has changed
My desires in life are no longer the same
My old friends look at me and say that I'm lame
They laugh at me and even call me strange

I pray for them because they really don't understand yet
That the love I have for this man in my heart has been set
I love the life that I'm living today
I'm learning more about Jesus each and every day
Since I met him remarkable things keep happening for me
And my life just keeps getting better indeed

When I go through my storms
I come out better
Because with Jesus, whatever I do, I'm always better!
If you're tired of mediocracy, try him and see
How much better your life can be

My testimony is that since Jesus came into my life
I'm just getting better each day
Looking back, I wouldn't have it any other way
Try Jesus for yourself
Let Him into your heart and you'll soon say
I'm Better! I'm Better! I'm Better Today!

2 Corinthians 5:17

Salvation

My life was dark and filled with sin
I wasn't really living my best life or trying to win
I thought I was enjoying the life I was living
And I had no reason to be forgiven

One day I heard a Word that convicted me
That Word grasped hold of me and wouldn't let me be
My eyes began to open, the scales fell off and I started to see
That God is my Savior and I needed to be set free

So I went to church and I heard the Word of the preacher say
There is a man named Jesus that created for you a new life... a new way
He will forgive you of every sin
And a new life for you, today, can began

The Word that I heard that day started bothering me
There was a tugging in my heart
And a feeling that I really wanted to be set free
Sin fought hard to hold me in my seat that day
But I couldn't shake this new feeling off of me, it wouldn't go away.

Before I knew it, I ran down to the altar and fell on my knees
I told that old preacher to pray for me please
I told him starting today that I want to be free
And the preacher said "Please pray the prayer of Salvation with me"

At that moment something strange started happening to me
Repentant tears began to fall
The name of Jesus I began to call
My hands began to raise
I was giving Him a mighty praise
There was a burning in my heart
And a feeling I never wanted to depart

I felt lighter as the chains of sin and bondage began to break
My hands were lifted and they began to shake
I knew that I was being set free
And that the chains that held me had fallen off of me

That day my life was changed forever
I don't want to go back to that old life, no never!
My heart felt lighter
And my continence was much brighter
Because sin no longer had a hold on me
The man named Jesus had set me free!
If you're in sin and you want to be free try Jesus
He'll do for you what he did for me

John 8:36, 2 Corinthians 5:17

Preachers, Preach!

To those of you who are called to preach my Word
Keep on preaching
Let your voice be heard
Lift up your voice like a trumpet sound
Let it be heard all around
Show all the people their transgression
Let them know that for their sins they must give a confession

Preach my word on the mountain top
And preach it in the valleys below
Preach my word faithfully
Wherever you are sent to go
Though you may get weary and you may get tired
Know that you are filled with my Holy Ghost Fire
You cannot stop because I have called you to preach
You have a world of lost souls you are assigned to reach

Be instant in season and out of season
Let the people know their sin
I died for that reason
So let your work begin

Reprove, rebuke, reprimand in love
Be enduring as I strengthen you from above
You are my special instrument, chosen and true
Oh! How I love to hear the sound that's inside of you

The sound of your trumpet when you speak
Has delivered many who were once considered weak
Those who were once lost, oppressed and bound
Heard the sound of your voice and are now set free and are found

I have anointed you and placed you as a shepherd over my sheep
Oh, how beautiful the eternal reward you will reap
In heaven I have prepared you a special seat
Because you did not succumb to the enemy
But you brought him to defeat

Preacher, there is a special reward in Heaven waiting for you
And a golden crown of Glory too
I have not forgotten all the sacrifice and work that you've done
I saw how you willingly, caringly, faithfully, and lovingly,
led my sheep to my Beloved Son
For now, Keep on preaching, Preacher Preach!
You have a world of souls you still have to teach

Isaiah 58:1

Reflection

You Will See Me Again

Think about your loved ones who have went home to Glory. They have escaped from the corruption and wickedness of this world and are now resting in the presence of God. They are now the happiest that they have ever been. They don't have a worry or a care. They are completely healed; sickness and disease does not even exist where they are. Imagine living in Heaven and the streets are paved with gold and filled with mansions that you have never dreamed of, and experiencing happiness and good health all the time, wanting for nothing, and never dying again.

God made this promise to us. He said "that one day His son is coming back to take His children home away from this evil world, so that we can be where He is forever". He told us His return will be a Great and Glorious Day for His children. The trumpet will sound and His children who are now resting will rise from the dead, the skies will split open, and Jesus will descend through the clouds with those who have died in Him.

This day is coming sooner than we think. Think about how you will feel when you see Jesus and your resurrected loved ones coming to take you to your new eternal home. Describe some of your feelings that you might feel on that Great Day.

_____

_____

_____

_____

_____

_____

Exercise Faith

We all have things that we are waiting on, hoping for or expecting in our lives. Sometimes the things that we are believing God for seems impossible to us. But we must remember that with God all things are possible. Faith is having complete confidence and assurance in the things that God has promised you. Faith is an unwavering belief that we SHALL receive even though our eyes have yet to see it. We must continue to reach for the things that seem impossible and that we wouldn't achieve. Trust God. Hold on to your faith that you have received through His word. Regardless of how long it may seem, we must trust in Him and have Faith in order to receive. EXERCISE YOUR FAITH TODAY!

Make a list of some of the things that you are believing God for in your life, and describe how you are exercising your faith.

_____

_____

_____

_____

_____

_____

_____

When God Speaks

Every word that God speaks is purposeful and intentional. God's word is absolute authority. Whatever He speaks happens. His word will never come back to Him unfulfilled. You can rest assured that whatever He has spoken to you it will definitely come to past in His timing. God never speaks a dead word. His words always bring life into every situation.

Make a list of some of the things that God has spoken to you. Are you still standing on His Word?

_____

_____

_____

_____

_____

_____

_____

People May Say

Sometimes people will say negative and cruel things to stop or hinder you from moving in the direction that God is taking you. People will say mean things about you. Their words are specifically designed to paralyze you and cause you to doubt who you really are. But when God speaks a word over you, His word supersedes what all others have to say. God never speaks a negative word over His creation because everything that He created is good. You are His creation, so when people have negative things to say about you, remember that you are so much more than what they say. Believe the word that God has already spoken over you!

Think about some of the negative things that people have spoken to you, rewrite that list with things that God has said about you.

_____

_____

_____

_____

_____

_____

_____

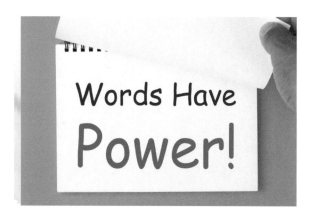

Today I Will Smile

There are some things that happen in our lives that is just out of our control. These things can sometimes weigh heavily on us and cause our continence to be woeful and distressed. Good News! You have the ability to choose to be happy or stressed. When you choose to have a joyful heart there's an inward healing that starts to take place inside of you. Putting a smile on your face seems simple but yet it is so powerful. Being cheerful heals the soul, like medicine cures the body of disease. It lifts the spirit and causes you to forget about the things you can't control. A smile not only brings joy into your heart, but it brings happiness to those around you. So, the next time that you are faced with weighty challenges look at them and laugh, and say to yourself "Today I Will Smile".

Which of these adjectives describes your joyful heart?

1.
2.
3.

READ Proverbs 15:13; Proverbs 17:22 and unscramble the scripture verse below. Write the correct scripture that corresponds with the correct chapter and verse.

Proverbs_____:_____
cheerful A spirit maketh a but countenance: merry by sorrow heart the of the heart is broken.

Proverbs _____:_____
medicine bones A good merry drieth the doeth like a; But a broken spirit.

Are you smiling TODAY?

Keep Moving On

Our aspirations and goals can look so unobtainable that sometimes it seems like we will never apprehend them because they seem so far out of our reach. One lesson that life teaches us, is that if we never go after our dreams, we will never achieve them. It doesn't matter how long it takes for us to reach the goals, but what matters most is that we remain focused, go after them, keep moving and striving towards them. As long as we are moving in their direction, we are making progress. It takes determination to conquer our goals and dreams no matter how big or challenging they may seem. If we trust God, continue to work hard, and remain diligent we will achieve what we strive toward. But we must keep moving forward. It doesn't matter whether we are making small steps or strides, we will reach the mountain top if we believe.

Write some of your goals that seems challenging for you right now. List some of the steps that you can do to move in the direction of achieving them.

_____

_____

_____

_____

_____

_____

_____

Just Try

We all have been blessed with certain gifts and talents that God has given to us individually. Many times, they lay dormant until we face circumstances that pull them out of us. This can cause us to feel a little uncertain and unsure of the gifts that we really have. As a result, we lose our confidence to "try". Gifts are not developed overnight. We must work on them in order to develop and perfect them. If we fail to push them out into the world, then the gifts will never be birthed out of us. If our gifts are not birthed, then we will never know what we can do or see the impact that our gifts will have on others. When you give your gifts and talents to God there is nothing that you can't do or accomplish but first you must "try", then your gift will make room for you.

Think about the gifts and talents that God has given to you. Make a list of some of the things that you can try today to develop and strengthen your gifts.

_____

_____

_____

_____

_____

_____

_____

You Can Make It Through

We all have times in which our faith has been tested and tried. On many occasions we exit one test and we enter another one. During these times we feel as if we're in a storm and can't see our way out. We feel as if God has abandoned us, but God never puts us in a storm and walks away from us. He is always right there leading and guiding us into brighter horizons. The only thing that you have to do is trust Him and believe that He knows what He is doing in your life. As long as you trust God, you will not only obtain victory, but you will not come out of the storm the same way that you entered into it. You will come out more refined, stronger and blessed.

Think about some of the test and trials that you have endured. Tell how they have made you better and describe how they turned out to be a Blessing for you.

_____

_____

_____

_____

_____

_____

_____

You Are A Vision

When people ask us who we are, we often identify ourselves by our career, sex, race or preconceived notions that others have placed on us. You are crafted by the hand of the Almighty God. He saw you in His mind long before you were conceived. He put Himself in you, and made you more special than all creation, because He loved you. You are unique. God created you exactly how He envisioned you and He preordained every step of your life. You are the manifestation of His vision. Now, when people ask you who you are: tell them that you are a Masterpiece created by God's Hand. You Are A Vision!

Think about the image that you have of yourself. What three things can you do to improve your image. Now, think about how God sees you. Write three positive proclamations about how you see yourself as God sees you and three steps to move you toward that vision.

Three things you can do to improve the way you see yourself.

1.
2.
3.

Three steps to move you toward that vision.

1.
2.
3.

See Yourself As God Sees You

Never allow the enemy to make you believe that you are worthless and that your life doesn't matter. You have been purchased with the Blood of Jesus Christ, and that makes you priceless. There is a very high value placed on your life. Your price is far greater that what anyone in this world can ever pay or afford. God stamped His seal of approval upon you when He saved you and made you brand new. Think of the great love that He has for you. He gave His only son to die, so that you can have eternal life. You are royal, precious and so beautiful in God's eyes. So, see yourself through His loving eyes. He paid a significant price for you so you can see yourself as He sees you.

Think about the view that you have of yourself.

Name three things that God did for you to prove your worth so you can now see yourself as God sees you.

1.
2.
3.

When you look at yourself through God's eyes what do you see?

1.
2.
3.

Mother of Zion

It's nothing like having a Godly Mother in your life to help teach you the ways of the Lord. Their life is a testimony of enduring faith and strength. If you listen to what they have to say you will learn a lot of valuable lessons. They have so much wisdom to impart and many stories to tell you about their Christian walk. So, open up your heart and grasp hold of a true Mother of Zion. You will find that she is invaluable to your Christian walk.

What does the Bible tell the older women to do in the book of Titus 2: 3-4

The _ _ _ _ wo_ _ _ likewise, _ _ _t th_y b_ in _ _ h_ _ _ _ _r as becometh h_ l_ _ _ _ _, not _a_s_ accusers, _ _ t g_v_ _ t_ m_c_ wine, _ea_ _ e_s of _o_d t_i_g_;

Th_t they _ _ y t_ _c_ the y_ _ _ _ w_ _ _ _t_ be _ _ b _ r, to _ _ _ e their h_ _ _ _ _s, _ _ l_ _ _ th_ _ r c_i_ _ _ _n,

The_ _ _ _ _ Wo_ _ _ _ likewise, _ _ _ _ t th _ y b_ in

What does the Bible say about those who are planted in the house of the Lord in Psalms 92:14?

T_ _ _ s_ _ ll still _r_ _ _ _ f _r _ _ fruit _ _ o_ _ _ g_; _h_y shall _ _f_ _ a_d _ _ _ _r_ _ _ _n_.

The Amazing Wonderful Woman

Woman you are so amazing. Everything about you was created wonderfully, from the way that you look, to the length of your hair, and the shape of your body. God made you beautiful. When He created you He didn't make a mistake. You are like a rare flower, in the midst of a beautiful garden, you stand out beautifully for everyone to see. There's a gracefulness, poise, and confidence about you that captivates the hearts of those around you. God thought so much about you that He created you out of the love of His heart. He made you special and He gave you the gentler part of His heart. You are full of intelligence, wit, and charm. With everything that you are, there is no reason for you to put yourself down. Woman you got it going on!

As women many times we often struggle with the image that we have about ourselves. Think about the image that you have about yourself and answer the following questions:

What does God's word say about you in Psalms 139:14?

I _ _ _ _ _ _ _ _ _ _ _ _ _; _r_ _ _ _ _ m_ _ _

NOW, List three areas about yourself in which you feel that doesn't line up to what God says about you.

1.
2.
3.

Name three constructive things that you can do to move you towards being the Amazing Wonderful Woman that you are

1.
2.
3.

LIFE IS BEAUTIFUL

Made To Be You

You were made to be "YOU." When God created you, He made you different. He didn't design you to be like anyone else in the whole wide world. Think about that! God made you unique and there is no one else in the whole world like you. When you are trying to be like someone else, what you are really saying to God is, I am not happy with the way that you made me to be. God didn't make a mistake with you. He knew everything about you, and the gifts and talents that He placed inside you, before you were born. So, embrace your individuality and love who you are. When God made you, He made you special. He made you to be a shining star.

Think about your personality and how special and unique you are:

List three things that stands out and shines about you.

1.
2.
3.

Tell how you use or will use your uniqueness/talents/gifts to bless others?

1.
2.
3.

I Always Win

The devil often thinks that he has power and control over us. He constantly throws things at us trying to catch us off guard. His main and ultimate goal is to trick and deceive us into doing what he wants us to do, by causing us to ignore and walk away from God. Satan wants us to abandon what God has called us to do because he is fearful, not only of God, but us too. The devil is a defeated foe and he has no power over you or your life. Satan lost all of his authority and power over you when you became washed in the blood of the lamb and said "yes" to God. He knows that he lost his power over you. The reason why he keeps coming back bothering you is that he is trying to reclaim you, he wants you back, but he can't have you. Satan is the bully that starts the fight, but you are the "Winner" who wins the fight. Because with Jesus every time you "show up" You Always Win.

Write at least two scriptures that you personally use to overcome the attacks of the enemy.

1.
2.

Below are steps that leads towards your pathway to victory against the enemy ... We always win when we use the weapons that God has given us. Some of those weapons are listed in the box below. Place each weapon on a step in the order that you use them to win the battle against the enemy in your current battle.

Pathway
to Victory

Praise, The Name of Jesus, Rebuke the enemy,
Pray, Use the Word of God, Resist the enemy, Fasting

Glad To See One More Day

It's a blessing to see a new day, to be alive and among the land of the living. We must never take God's mercy and grace for granted because tomorrow is not promised to any of us. Many people did not wake up to see a new day, but God gave you another day. Every day that you wake up, you are blessed. Life is a gift given from God, no one knows the number of his days. So be grateful for another day of life, and the opportunities that a day may bring. Enjoy the occasions you've been given today. Rejoice and be glad because today is an adventurous, beautiful, wonderful, brand-new day. And most of all give God thanks because He has allowed you to see One More Day.

Fill in the circle with reasons why you are glad to see another day

Now, connect those reasons with ways that you can show God your gratitude for life.

Reasons I'm glad to see another day

Ways to show God my gratitude for life.

Do you see the Connection?

Use your reasons to show God your gratitude every day.

Morning Praise

God loves our praise. Every day that you are blessed with a new day you ought to give God praise. He didn't have to bless you with another day, but because He was kind to you, you ought to stop and take time to worship Him. Think about what He has done for you, how He has given you new mercy, new grace and blessings. Worship is one way that we can show our appreciation to God for what He has done for us. So everyday remember to get up and worship God and thank Him for all that He has done for you.

<u>Acts of Worship:</u>

Use the Words in the box to complete the seek and find puzzle.

Magnify	Glorify
Adoration	Sing
Praises	Thanksgiving

```
C Y A U H B M W S W Z T N Y W
A U F V D A H E Y V C M D R K
A Z U I G M S B T E X I S Y F
H Q Y N R I V N T C U X M A M
N V I X A O A D O R A T I O N
G F T R A M L V K P Y F I I K
Y B P G C X Z G U C J F I I I
W U L W T Q D T Y G V S O S D
K H C M Q E N J V M S A Z N I
Q R G P R I L J L U E Q V B N
G N I V I G S K N A H T G W F
K Z A F R Z E Q X Q I Z N X V
G I V J D E J J K L C P I J R
F Z J I S X C E D F G H S T A
T F R Z A K P G B K S T W D R
```

In His Presence

Morning prayer is like a sweet aroma to God. It is nothing like being in His presence early in the morning and being surrounded by His peace. I love those quiet times spent with God when you come secretly before Him and pour out your heart, or you wait in silence for Him to speak, or when songs of praises just flow from your heart. Wow! Those intimate moments with God are so special. He's the best friend that you can always confide in. You can talk to him about anything as long as you like. He's never in a rush, He's always waiting for you to tell Him what's on your mind so that He can answer you, guide you, and put joy within your heart. When you're in God's presence there's so many good things that He reveals to you. He loads you with daily benefits and blessings because your prayer has touched His heart.

Think about your prayer life. Do you have a consistent time set aside in which you seek God? If you are struggling in this area, below are some steps that you can take in order to strengthen your prayer life.

Steps to a Better Prayer Life:

1. Set aside a time in which you will pray to God every morning
2. Don't let anything distract you from your prayer time
3. Be consistent with your prayer time. Practice it consistently every day for at least 15 minutes
4. Listen to the voice of God

To form a habit, it often takes 21 days of doing something consistently. Practice steps 1-4 for the next 21 days. Then, describe how your prayer life has changed since you have used the above steps in your daily pray life.

_____

_____

_____

_____

Describe a moment when you were in the presence of GOD and tell how you will hold on to His presence.

_____

_____

_____

_____

God's Grace

In your Christian walk sometimes, you may fall or miss the mark, but that is no reason for you to give up. If you come to God with a sorrowful heart and ask for His forgiveness, He will forgive and restore you. God never wants you to fall. His desire is that you come through every test and trial victoriously. But God knows that because you are human that there are times that you will make mistakes and fall short. God's love for His people is so strong that He allows an open opportunity for us to come before His throne of grace and seek forgiveness and find His mercy. Isn't it good to know that you can come before God and don't have to feel ashamed about your failures and sins? Once you confess your sins to God, He throws them into the sea of forgetfulness and He remembers them no more. But the devil tries to keep you trapped in your past sins and failures. He tries to make you think that God has not forgiven you, but the devil is a liar. When God forgives you, you are forgiven and there are no questions about it. However, you must be careful NOT to take God's Grace and forgiveness for granted. You must keep yourself free from all iniquity and repetitive sin, if you don't you will pay a costly price for your sin.

We all have things in our life that we need God's forgiveness for. It could be something as simple as disobedience or procrastination, etc. Think about those hidden areas in your life, have you taken them to the Throne of Grace?

Think about it. Name 2 things in which you need to repent for:

1.
2.

Pray for forgiveness in those areas. God's Grace has now forgiven you.

Every time that God forgives you of something and you don't go back to it, you have gained VICTORY over that area of your life.

Think about it. Name three things in your life that you have gained victory over in your life

1.
2.
3.

Now, Rejoice! God's Grace has set you free!

Use Your Talents

The parable of The Talents

We all have talents that God has given to us according to our ability. God desires that we use them for His edification no matter how small they may seem in our eyes. If we give our talents back to God they will increase. God is always interested in bringing increase into our lives. But He cannot increase what we have not given to Him. Don't minimize the gift that you have been given by comparing your gift to the gift of others. God wants you to work with what you have by developing and using what He has given unto you. If you hide the talents and gifts that He has given to you then they lay dormant and will never grow. When you choose not to use what God has given to you, it's like you're saying to God that you don't appreciate what He has given you. This angers and displeases God. Every talent or gift that God has entrusted you with is very important no matter how big or small it may seem. How can God trust you with a lot if you don't use the little talent that you got? God is watching and will judge you on what you do with what He has given you. When you don't use what God has given to you He will take it away from you and give it to someone else.

Read Matthew 25:14-30 and fill in the missing words

For the Kingdom of heaven is as a man traveling into a far country, who called his own servants, and delivered unto him his [   ] Unto one he gave five [   ] to another two, and to another [   ] to every man according to his several ability; and straightway took his journey.

Then he that has received the five [   ] talents went and traded with the same, and made them other [   ] [   ].

And likewise he that had received [   ] he also [   ] other [   ]

But he that had received one went and [   ] in the earth, and [   ] his [   ] money.

After a long time the Lord of those servants came and [   ] with them.

The Lord said unto his servant who had been given the five talents and to the one who had been given two talents well done good and [＿＿＿＿＿＿＿＿] servant; thou hast been [＿＿＿＿＿＿＿＿] over a few things, I will make you ruler over [＿＿＿＿＿＿＿＿] things.

But to the servant who hid his talent the Lord said unto him thou wicked and [＿＿＿＿＿＿＿＿] servant.

Shine Your Light

Light shines its brightest in the darkest hour. We are truly living in a world that is full of darkness because of sin. People are in despair, feeling lost, hopeless, and looking for something true that they can trust and believe in. They are seeking answers for how to live in this world today. As children of God, we must step up and do our part, by not being afraid to share what God has done for us. We must tell them the story of Jesus love and how He died for them. We must open up our hearts and let God's unconditional love flow through so that the people can see Jesus through us. As children of God, we must let our light shine brightly wherever we go and in whatever we do.

Plugged In and Turned On

"You are the light of the world." Matthew 5:14 (NIV)
Based on Matthew 5:14-16 (NIV)

```
X V F O K U L Y B D S M M O I
M J M B Y D T G Y Q E S X Z A
M Z V M L I E O S L R E L Z R
L P A R C S N O L H L P D I O
I Z V K I C Y D F W I H B S I
G L D A A V S F L Y P N B R F
H B R D K N A W O R L D E Z B
T P I O O H I D D E N E R H L
B C V B O W L T M B S K V C A
O N H P U L A M P U O S X U C
T Y F I J T X R O F P L C V J
P R J D L J I H A Y B C F W R
E I Q L X L E F A T H E R E V
C F M E N S N M U V Z W O B A
X I L R M D R J L I S T A N D
```

LAMP	LIGHT	BOWL	GOOD	DEEDS
WORLD	CITY	MEN	HIDDEN	SHINE
PRAISE	HOUSE	FATHER	HILL	STAND

Negative Thoughts

We all have thoughts that come to our mind that does not line up with the word of God. If we are not careful those thoughts will overwhelm and overtake us, by causing us to dwell on unprofitable things. Negative, evil, anxious, depressive, and unhappy thoughts will grow if we allow them to sit in our hearts. It is important that we purge our thoughts to keep our hearts clean and pure before God. As God's children we can't accept just any thought that comes to our mind. We must constantly guard our mind and rebuke wrong thinking by renewing our mind daily with God's word, and thinking on things according to God's way. If we don't learn to control our thoughts, they will lead to wrong emotions and guide our actions.

This is why we must immediately take captive and cast down every wrong thought that comes to our mind.

Draw a Line and Match each word in the box to its best description

1. If you are trustworthy you are
2. To be morally right
3. Something that is praiseworthy
4. The book of Philippians 4:8 talks about
5. Another word for honest
6. Something that is admirable is
7. If it is uncontaminated, it is
8. The opposite of a bad report

| Our Thinking |
| Lovely |
| Pure |
| Just |
| Good Report |
| Honest |
| Admirable |
| True |

Steps to encourage right thinking.
Match the scripture to the correct book listed below.

_____ And be not conformed to this world: but be ye transformed by the renewing of your mind, that ye may prove what is that good, and acceptable, and perfect will of God.

_____ Casting down Imaginations, and every high thing that exhalteth itself against the knowledge of God, and bringing into captivity every thought to the obedience of Christ.

_____ As He thinketh in his heart so is he;

A. Proverbs 23:7
B. Romans 12:2
C. 2 Corinthians 10:5

What do you think?

I'm Better

The day that Jesus came into your life everything changed. You are not the same person that you use to be, but you are a new creature. You are born again. God has made everything about you brand new. You are now a much "Better" person than you were before you met Christ. Your old self has been crucified with Christ and a new and "Better" you have been resurrected. You now have God's spirit living inside of you, and God's peace and joy dwells in you. When your unsaved friends look at you, they do not understand the drastic change that has come over you, so they often laugh, criticize or they may even avoid you, because you don't do the same things that you use to do. Since Jesus came into your life, your whole world changed and things just keep getting BETTER and BETTER for you.

Write your answers on the appropriate side of the scale.

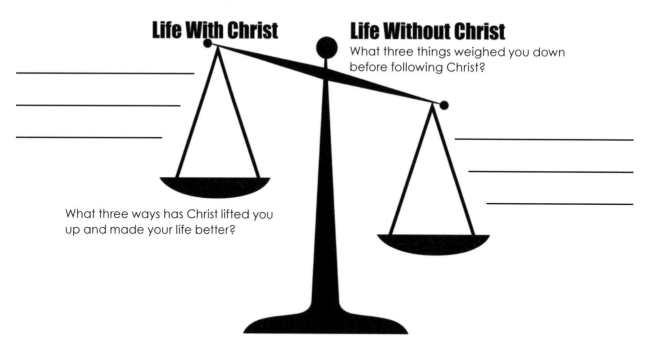

Life With Christ

Life Without Christ
What three things weighed you down
before following Christ?

What three ways has Christ lifted you
up and made your life better?

Don't be the same
Be better!

Salvation

Think about the time before Jesus entered into your heart. Maybe you thought that you were living a good life. Maybe you were searching for hope, for peace, happiness, or searching for your purpose in life. Perhaps you were doing things to make your life feel fulfilled only to return to emptiness and unfulfillment. Maybe, there was a void that you just couldn't fill. To those looking on the outside, you looked as if you were doing fine, but your life was really an internal mess. One day something changed because you heard about God's love, and of how He can set you free. And make your life brand new. You decided to give Him a try by repenting of your sins and asking Him to live inside of your heart. Remember the day and the moment that Jesus entered into your heart? Remember, how much lighter and happier you felt when your sins were washed away and the chains of sin and bondage were broken off of you. Today, you are living free from your old ways of life and living a brand-new life in Christ. The day that you accepted Jesus was the best day of your life! That day was your day of Salvation.

Read John 8:36 and write what God's Word says about being free.

_____

_____

_____

Read 2 Corinthians 5:17
Now, unscramble the scripture 2 Corinthians 5:17 below

Erotheref fi nya mna eb ni rhcsit eh si a ewn erutcrea; Ido snigth era ssedap yawa; belohd, lla sgniht rea wen.

_____

_____

_____

**SALVATION – YOU ARE NOW FREE
FROM THE SHACKLES OF SIN**

Words from the Heart
A Message from the Author

I started this process not really knowing what I was getting into or what I was doing. I thought that writing a book of poetry was just pulling old writings together from the closet shelf, dusting them off and putting them into a book. Boy, was I ever wrong! The first sample that I produced for this project did not quite meet the mark. I learned that I was missing important elements that needed to be conveyed. Upon learning this I felt like a failure and I wanted to quit.

Later, I asked God, "Why did you give me these things if you never wanted me to use them, and why did you let me get this far in the process if you did not want me to go further? God answered me through a wise man who looked over my project and shared with me the things that I was missing and gave me some pointers on how to move forward. He also encouraged me and emphatically told me, "You can't quit, you have to finish this project". He stated to me that, "You have to start somewhere."I took his words to heart and began working diligently as new inspiration began to pour into me. The journey was long, and I completed several rough drafts before I had a finished product in which I felt confident. There were times in this process that I wanted to give up because it was easier for me to quit than to keep moving forward. But I was inspired to continue on. I would wake up in the morning hearing words and would go to bed hearing words. There were times that I was awake in the early hours of the morning writing. A thought or phrase would come to mind, and I had no clue of what I was going to write next, so I had to wait until the next thought was given before I could go forward. Nevertheless, I kept working diligently and before I knew it, I had completed my task and reached my goal.

I say to you, as you go through your journey in life, whether you're in times of testing, times of construction, times of grieving, or whatever place or season that you're experiencing, there's always hope and a brighter day for every situation, and for everything that you are facing.

Don't let obstacles or hindrances get in your way. If you trust God, he will always lead you to victory. Whatever call, talents and gifts that you have, I encourage you to use them, give them back to God as he has given them to you. You will be surprised of the many things that you can do. There is a beautiful gift blooming inside of you!

Be Inspired and Encouraged

About the Author

Rhonda received her education through the Detroit Public School System.

Her passion and drive to be acceptable to God gave her a desire to reach and help other people. Following that passion, she obtained her Master's Degree in Social Work from the University of Michigan, with a Major in Social Work Administration and Minor in Interpersonal (Clinical) Practices. She is a Licensed Social Worker within the state of Michigan, and have served in many capacities within her field.

Throughout her career she never ceased to tell others about the love and saving grace of God. Through witnessing and testimony her desire is to touch the lives of many. She is a member of Perfecting Church in Detroit, Michigan under the leadership of Bishop Marvin L. Winans, Sr.

As a teenager, in her quiet time she was often writing her thoughts and feelings on paper. At the age of 16 she shared that God was going to allow her to write a book someday.

Well, here it is.

Printed in the United States
by Baker & Taylor Publisher Services